CONTEN

THE COVENANT SERVICE

INTRODUCTION

From the earliest days of the Methodist societies, John Wesley invited the Methodist people to renew their covenant relationship with God. Wesley drew much of his material for the service from seventeenth-century Puritans and subsequently made changes to it. The Wesleyan Conference revised it twice during the nineteenth century and other branches of Methodism had versions of it.

The Book of Offices (1936) included a form of *The Covenant Service* which quickly achieved great popularity. **The Methodist Service Book** (1975) version strengthened the link between the renewal of the covenant and the Holy Communion, but at the cost of losing some familiar and much loved passages. In the present service, some of these have been recast and restored, not least in the penitential section.

The present *Covenant Service* moves from praise of the Trinity to listening to the word in scripture, read and preached, and then follows a penitential approach to the words of the Covenant. Changes in the use and understanding of language have led to the provision of two forms of this part of the service. The first form is offered as a contemporary version of the Covenant Prayer; the second form is the more traditional text. In this form, the words, 'Put me to doing, put me to suffering', have raised difficulties for some people. These words do not mean that we ask God to make us suffer, but rather that we desire, by God's help, actively to do or patiently to accept whatever is God's will for us.

The emphasis of the whole service is on God's readiness to enfold us in generous love, not dependent on our deserving. Our response, also in love, springs with penitent joy from thankful recognition of God's grace. The covenant is not just a one-to-one transaction between individuals and God, but the act of the whole faith community. The prayers of intercession which follow emphasize our unity with all humanity. The service proceeds to the Lord's Supper, for which a special form has been provided to emphasize the continuity between word, response and sacrament. The service is meant to lead us, by a path both similar to and differing from that of normal Sunday worship, to that commitment which all worship seeks both to inspire and to strengthen.

NOTES

1 *The Covenant Service* should normally be held only once in each year.

2 At whatever time of day this service is held, it should be regarded as the principal service and used in full.

THE GATHERING OF THE PEOPLE OF GOD

1 Hymn

[handwritten: 99 As with gladness men of old]

2   Let us pray.

Glory to the Father, the God of love,
who created us;
who continually preserves and sustains us;
who has loved us with an everlasting love,
and given us the light of the knowledge of his glory
in the face of Jesus Christ.

Blessèd be God for ever.

Glory to Jesus Christ our Saviour,
who, though he was rich,
yet for our sake became poor,
and was tested in every way as we are,
yet without sin;

who proclaimed the good news of the kingdom,
and was obedient to the point of death,
even death on a cross;
who was raised from the dead and is alive for ever,
and has opened the kingdom of heaven
to all who trust in him;
who is seated at God's right hand in glory,
and will come to be our judge.

Blessèd be God for ever.

Glory to the Holy Spirit,
the Lord, the giver of life,
by whom we are born into the family of God,
and made members of the body of Christ;
whose witness confirms us;
whose wisdom teaches us;
whose power enables us;
who will do for us more than we can ask or think.

Blessèd be God for ever.

To the one God, Father, Son and Holy Spirit,
be praise and glory for ever. **Amen.**

3 Silence

4 Collect

God of grace,
through the mediation of your Son,
you call us into a new covenant.
Help us therefore to draw near with faith
and join ourselves in a perpetual covenant with you;
through Jesus Christ our Lord. **Amen.**

THE MINISTRY OF THE WORD

5   A reading from the Law.

Exodus 24:3-11 *or* Deuteronomy 29:10-15 is read.

For the wisdom that guides us
we praise you, O God.

6   A reading from the Prophets.

Jeremiah 31:31-34 is read.

For the word that inspires us
we praise you, O God.

7   A reading from the Epistles.

Romans 12:1-2 is read.

For the truth that enlightens us
we praise you, O God.

8   Hymn   *82 Glad music fills the Christmas sky*

9   A reading from the Gospel according to . . .

Hear the Gospel of Christ.
Glory to Christ our Saviour.

The Gospel, John 15:1-10 *or* Mark 14:22-25, is read.

This is the Gospel of Christ.
Praise to Christ our Lord.

10 Sermon

11 Hymn   *HP| 649 in Hymns & Psalms p. 287. on this book*

THE COVENANT

12   God made a covenant with the people of Israel, calling them to be a holy nation, chosen to bear witness to his steadfast love by finding delight in the law.

The covenant was renewed in Jesus Christ our Lord, in his life, work, death and resurrection. In him all people may be set free from sin and its power, and united in love and obedience.

In this covenant God promises us new life in Christ. For our part we promise to live no longer for ourselves but for God.

We meet, therefore, as generations have met before us, to renew the covenant which bound them and binds us to God.

Let us then seek forgiveness for the sin by which we have denied God's claim upon us.

13   Let us pray.

God of mercy, hear us as we confess our sins.

For the sin that has made us slow to learn from Christ,
reluctant to follow him,
and afraid to bear the cross:

Lord, have mercy,
Lord, forgive.

For the sin that has caused the poverty of our worship,
the formality and selfishness of our prayers,
our neglect of fellowship and the means of grace,
and our hesitating witness for Christ:

Lord, have mercy,
Lord, forgive.

Philip to lead

For the sin that has led us to misuse your gifts,
evade our responsibilities,
and fail to be good stewards of your creation:

Lord, have mercy,
Lord, forgive.

For the sin that has made us unwilling to overcome evil
    with good,
tolerant of injustice,
quick to condemn,
and selfish in sharing your love with others:

Lord, have mercy,
Lord, forgive.

Silence

**Have mercy on me, O God,
in your constant love;
in the fullness of your mercy
blot out my offences.
Wash away all my guilt,
and cleanse me from my sin.
Create in me a clean heart, O God,
and renew a right spirit within me.
Give me the joy of your help again
and strengthen me with a willing spirit.**

The presiding minister says:

If we confess our sins,
God is faithful and just,
and will forgive our sins,
and cleanse us from all unrighteousness.

Therefore to all who truly repent
this is his gracious word:
'Your sins are forgiven.'

Amen. Thanks be to God.

Philip to lead

14 Hymn

> **Come, let us use the grace divine,**
> **And all, with one accord,**
> **In a perpetual cov'nant join**
> **Ourselves to Christ the Lord:**

> **Give up ourselves, through Jesu's power,**
> **His name to glorify;**
> **And promise, in this sacred hour,**
> **For God to live and die.**

> **The cov'nant we this moment make**
> **Be ever kept in mind:**
> **We will no more our God forsake,**
> **Or cast his words behind.**

> **We never will throw off his fear**
> **Who hears our solemn vow;**
> **And if thou art well pleased to hear,**
> **Come down, and meet us now.**

> **To each the cov'nant blood apply,**
> **Which takes our sins away;**
> **And register our names on high,**
> **And keep us to that day.**

15 The people remain standing and the presiding minister says:

EITHER

A Sisters and brothers in Christ,
   let us again accept our place within this covenant
   which God has made with us and with all who are called to
       be Christ's disciples.

   This means that, by the help of the Holy Spirit,
   we accept God's purpose for us,
   and the call to love and serve God
   in all our life and work.

Christ has many services to be done:
some are easy, others are difficult;
some bring honour, others bring reproach;
some are suitable to our natural inclinations and material
    interests,
others are contrary to both;
in some we may please Christ and please ourselves;
in others we cannot please Christ except by denying
    ourselves.
Yet the power to do all these things is given to us in Christ,
    who strengthens us.

Therefore let us make this covenant of God our own.
Let us give ourselves to him,
trusting in his promises and relying on his grace.

Eternal God,
in your faithful and enduring love
you call us to share in your gracious covenant in Jesus
    Christ.
In obedience we hear and accept your commands;
in love we seek to do your perfect will;
with joy we offer ourselves anew to you.
We are no longer our own but yours.

I am no longer my own but yours.
Your will, not mine, be done in all things,
    wherever you may place me,
    in all that I do
        and in all that I may endure;
    when there is work for me
        and when there is none;
    when I am troubled
        and when I am at peace.
Your will be done
    when I am valued
        and when I am disregarded;
    when I find fulfilment
        and when it is lacking;
    when I have all things,
        and when I have nothing.

I willingly offer
all I have and am
 to serve you,
 as and where you choose.

Glorious and blessèd God,
Father, Son and Holy Spirit,
 you are mine and I am yours.
 May it be so for ever.
 Let this covenant now made on earth
 be fulfilled in heaven. Amen.

OR

B Beloved in Christ,
   let us again claim for ourselves
   this covenant which God has made with his people,
   and take upon us the yoke of Christ.

   This means that we are content
   that he appoint us our place and work,
   and that he himself be our reward.

   Christ has many services to be done:
   some are easy, others are difficult;
   some bring honour, others bring reproach;
   some are suitable to our natural inclinations and material
     interests,
   others are contrary to both;
   in some we may please Christ and please ourselves;
   in others we cannot please Christ except by denying
     ourselves.
   Yet the power to do all these things is given to us in Christ,
     who strengthens us.

   Therefore let us make this covenant of God our own.
   Let us give ourselves to him,
   trusting in his promises and relying on his grace.

Lord God, holy Father,
since you have called us through Christ
to share in this gracious covenant,
we take upon ourselves with joy the yoke of obedience
and, for love of you,
engage ourselves to seek and do your perfect will.
We are no longer our own but yours.

I am no longer my own but yours.
Put me to what you will,
rank me with whom you will;
put me to doing,
    put me to suffering;
let me be employed for you
    or laid aside for you,
exalted for you
    or brought low for you;
let me be full,
    let me be empty,
let me have all things,
    let me have nothing;
I freely and wholeheartedly yield all things
to your pleasure and disposal.

And now, glorious and blessèd God,
Father, Son and Holy Spirit,
you are mine and I am yours.
So be it.
And the covenant now made on earth,
let it be ratified in heaven. Amen.

16 Silence, all seated

17   As we have entered this covenant not for ourselves alone,
      but as God's servants and witnesses, let us pray for the
      Church and for the world.

      Loving God, hear us as we pray for your holy catholic
          Church:
      make us all one, that the world may believe.

Inspire and lead all who govern and hold authority in the
    nations of the world:
establish justice and peace among all people.

Have compassion on all who suffer from any sickness,
    grief or trouble:
deliver them from their distress.

We praise you for all your saints who have entered your
    eternal glory:
bring us all to share in your heavenly kingdom.

Let us pray in silence for our own needs and for those of
others . . .

Silence

Lord our God,
you have helped us by your grace
to make these prayers,
and you have promised through Christ our Lord
that when two or three agree in his name
you will grant what they ask.
Answer now your servants' prayers
according to their needs;
in this world grant that we may truly know you,
and in the world to come
graciously give us eternal life;
through Jesus Christ our Lord. **Amen.**

THE LORD'S SUPPER

18 The Peace

All stand.

Susan to lead

The Lord has made an everlasting covenant of peace with
his people.

The peace of the Lord be always with you.
And also with you.

The people may greet one another in the name of Christ.

THE PREPARATION O 417 Lord Jesus Christ

19 Hymn

20 The offerings of the people are presented. Bread and wine are brought to the table (or if already on the table are uncovered). The presiding minister takes the bread and wine and prepares them for use.

THE THANKSGIVING

21 All stand.

The presiding minister leads the great prayer of thanksgiving:

The Lord be with you.
And also with you.

Lift up your hearts.
We lift them to the Lord.

Let us give thanks to the Lord our God.
It is right to give our thanks and praise.

God our Father, fountain of goodness,
creator of all that is,
you have made us in your own image.
You have given us life and reason,
and love for one another,
setting in our hearts a hunger for you.

In darkness you are our light,
in adversity and temptation our strength.
You bear patiently with our folly and sin,
granting us your law to guide us
and your prophets to renew our faith.

In the fullness of time
you came to us in love and mercy
in Jesus Christ, your living Word,
full of grace and truth.

He lived among us,
declaring your forgiveness
and revealing your wisdom
in works of mercy and in his word of power.
For us he suffered and died upon the cross,
by death destroying death.
You raised him from the dead
and exalted him to your right hand on high.
Through him you sent your Holy Spirit
to be the life and light of your people,
gathered together in every time and place
to glorify your holy name.

With them and all the company of heaven
we join in the unending hymn of praise:

Holy, holy, holy Lord,
God of power and might,
heaven and earth are full of your glory.
Hosanna in the highest.
Blessèd is he who comes in the name of the Lord.
Hosanna in the highest.

Holy God, pour out your Spirit
that these gifts of bread and wine
may be for us the body and blood
of your Son Jesus Christ our Lord,
who, on the night in which he was betrayed,
took bread, gave thanks, broke it,
and gave it to his disciples, saying,
'Take this and eat it.
This is my body given for you.
Do this in remembrance of me.'

In the same way, after supper,
he took the cup, gave thanks,
and gave it to them, saying,

'Drink from it, all of you.
This is my blood of the new covenant,
poured out for you and for many,
for the forgiveness of sins.
Do this, whenever you drink it,
in remembrance of me.'

Christ has died.
Christ is risen.
Christ will come again.

And so, Lord, we obey his command
with this bread and this cup,
by which we recall his death and resurrection,
the source of our life and salvation.
Grant that we, who share in this holy sacrament,
may be united by your Spirit
and grow into perfect love.

Bring us,
with those who have done your will in every age,
into the light of your presence
and the joy of your kingdom.

Through Christ, with Christ, in Christ,
in the power of the Holy Spirit,
we worship you in songs of everlasting praise.
Blessing and honour and glory and power
be yours for ever and ever. Amen.

22 The Lord's Prayer

EITHER

OR

We say together the prayer
that Jesus gave us:

As our Saviour taught his
disciples, we pray:

Our Father in heaven,
hallowed be your Name,
your kingdom come,
your will be done,
on earth as in heaven.

Our Father, who art in
heaven,
hallowed be thy Name;
thy kingdom come;
thy will be done;

Give us today our daily
   bread.
Forgive us our sins
as we forgive those who
   sin against us.
Save us from the time of
   trial
and deliver us from evil.
For the kingdom, the
   power and the glory
   are yours,
now and for ever. Amen.

on earth as it is in heaven.
Give us this day our
   daily bread.
And forgive us our
   trespasses,
as we forgive those who
   trespass against us.
And lead us not into
   temptation;
but deliver us from evil.
For thine is the kingdom,
   the power, and the
   glory,
for ever and ever. Amen.

THE BREAKING OF THE BREAD

23 The presiding minister breaks the bread in the sight of the
   people in silence, or saying:

   The things of God for God's holy people.

   Jesus Christ is holy;
   Jesus Christ is Lord.
   Glory to God the Father.

24 Silence, all seated or kneeling

THE SHARING OF THE BREAD AND WINE

25 The presiding minister, those assisting with the distribution,
   and the people receive, according to local custom.

   The presiding minister may invite the congregation to receive
   communion with these or similar words:

   Jesus said: 'I am the bread of life.
   Those who come to me shall not hunger
   and those who believe in me shall never thirst.'

   Draw near with faith.

26 Words such as the following are said during the distribution:

> The body of Christ keep you in eternal life. **Amen.**

> The blood of Christ keep you in eternal life. **Amen.**

27 During the distribution there may be appropriate music.

28 The elements that remain are covered with a white cloth.

PRAYERS AND DISMISSAL

29 Silence

30   Let us pray.

> **Faithful God,**
> **with these holy gifts**
> **you have fed and strengthened us**
> **in Jesus Christ your Son.**
> **Guide us on our way,**
> **that with all your faithful people**
> **we may come to share the feast**
> **of your eternal kingdom;**
> **through Jesus Christ our Lord. Amen.**

31 Hymn

328 Lord for the years

32 The presiding minister sa

> The blessing of God,
> the Father, the Son and the Holy Spirit,
> be upon *you/us* and remain with *you/us* for ever. **Amen.**

33 The presiding minister says:

> Go in peace to love and serve the Lord.

> **In the name of Christ. Amen.**

ACKNOWLEDGEMENTS

Every effort has been made to ensure that the following list of acknowledgements is as comprehensive as possible, but the experience of those involved in the preparation of **The Methodist Worship Book** is similar to that of the compilers of the **Book of Common Order** of the Church of Scotland, who state:

> Many sources have contributed to the compilation of this book, and not all of them are now traceable. Individual members of the Committee prepared drafts, which were revised more or less drastically by the Committee, often resulting in final versions which looked little like the original drafts. Among the casualties of this sometimes protracted process was the identity of many of the sources; they could not be recalled, nor did there seem to be any way to track them down. The Panel wishes to record at once both its indebtedness to any who may recognise in this book rhythms and patterns, expressions and phrases, ideas and images which are their own, and its regret that it became impossible to ask permission or seek consent for their inclusion . . .

> If, through inadvertence, copyright material has been used without permission or acknowledgement, the publisher will be grateful to be informed and will be pleased to make the necessary correction in subsequent editions.

The symbol * in the following paragraphs denotes that a text has been altered.

Except where indicated below, all psalms, scripture readings and scripture sentences are taken from **The New Revised Standard Version of the Bible (Anglicized Edition),** © 1989, 1995 by the Division of Christian Education of the National Council of Churches of Christ in the United States of America, and are used by permission. All rights reserved.

Some scripture sentences are from **The Revised Standard Version,** © 1946 and 1952 by the Division of Christian Education of the National Council of Churches of Christ in the United States of America, and are used by permission. All rights reserved.